Opening to the Knowledge

An artist's journey discovering the energy within nature.

Vol 8

Extract from the original book,

'A Glimpse in a Transient Zone'

Jo Eaton.

Copyright.

All rights reserved. No part of this book may be reproduced by any mechanical, photographic, or electronic process, or in the form of a phonographic recording; nor may it be stored in a retrieval system, transmitted, or otherwise be copied for public or private use - other than for 'fair use' as brief quotations embodied in articles and reviews - without prior written permission of the publisher.

Disclaimer.

The author of this book does not dispense medical advice or prescribe the use of any technique as a form of treatment for physical or medical problems without the advice of a physician, either directly or indirectly. The intent of the author is only to offer information of a general nature to help you in your quest for emotional and spiritual well-being. In the event you use any of the information in this book for yourself, which Is your constitutional right, the author and the publisher assume no responsibility for your actions.

In order to protect identity, I have changed the names of some of the characters within many of the stories.

Contents

Chapter 1. Introduction………………………………. 1

Chapter 2. Critical Studies: Attaining a Higher Level of Perception……………3

Chapter 3. Ancient Wisdoms…………………………..15

Chapter 4. The Importance of Communicating the Visual Image……………………17

Chapter 5. Energy Emitting from Nature………19

Chapter 6. Methodologies…………………………..21

Chapter 7. Continuing with the Artistic Quest………………………………………37

Chapter 1

Introduction

For years, I have been captivated by the sounds, rhythm of the seasons and the vibrations that celebrate Nature. It has been through working as an artist, in the landscape, that my perceptions developed and I realised that all of nature has the same life source energy, the flora, fauna and elements too, all vibrating in harmony as part of the cycle of life.

I feel in nature there are no edges and no solidity. Every small particle is a cluster of energy vibrating in an immense void. It appears there are infinite fields of energy, vibrating at different frequencies, ever flowing, ever changing, renewing and in a state of transformation. Each of us is connected by this energy source, including our environment. Every form is essentially energy, vibrating and in transition.

As an artist, I have a vision of communicating this essence of life within my work, through a variety of print processes, 3D installations and digital imagery.

Chapter 2

Critical Studies: Attaining a Higher Level of Perception

It was while I was studying for my Fine Art Degree, that I started to look more closely at the paintings of the great Masters. I began to realise that they had each attained a more advanced level of perception, a higher plane of consciousness, rather than the normal human range. The more in depth I studied each artist, the more I realised that this heightened awareness was surely attained through meditation. Throughout my thesis, I looked more closely at the work of Leonardo De Vinci, Monet and Rembrandt, to name a few, and each artist's works were so much more advanced for their time. Just looking at the progressive inventions of Leonardo, I believe he must have been having assistance through channelling from a higher domain, in order that he could create such advanced vehicles and inventions. In fact, not only great artists, but sculptors, musicians, poets, philosophers and architects etc. have each produced masterpieces for mankind. As stated by the Bulgarian philosopher Omraam Mikhael Aivanhov in his book, 'Creation: Artistic and Spiritual' about these creative genii:

> 'Before starting work, they recollected themselves and meditated and prayed for Heavenly blessings, for only Heaven can give us the light which illuminates the imagination. The result of this approach was that they

received the revelation of true beauty and were enabled to express and communicate it to others.'

It is when viewing such work of the Masters, it communicates that the artist has been inspired by a higher order, as you are experiencing something of the artists experience. This is the meaning of a true artist. One who is able to absorb and vibrate those particles, then communicate and enlighten this spiritual light through creativity. Aivanhov states that initiates, mystics and artists all have a positive influence on humanity through their aptitude to spread light, while in turn, progresses the development of the earth.

As an artist, I believe it is important to do a great amount of work on oneself, in order to project this clarity of beauty within one's work. As Omraam Mikhael Aivanhov stated:

'Obviously, if you want to give, you must first possess'.

Through my lengthy research, I have been aware of this intrinsic feature of vibrating energy within nature, which has acted as a catalyst to motivate artists to assess and review their experiences of our world. They have tried to emulate this power within their work, having been also greatly influenced by the increased scientific discoveries of our natural environment.

It is often difficult to separate the spiritual from the scientific, the aesthetic from the philosophical, when articulating your perceptions within nature. The laws of physics, quantum mechanics, relativity and antimatter are how Nature works, so it is inevitable the artist will represent and comment on these aspects of human life. Due to the present global climate, where the general mood is of an increased receptiveness to new ideas, self-development, world peace, and an awareness of environmental issues, not only ecologically but culturally too, this is a very emotive period for the artist, a wonderful opportunity to increase our creativity.

I have noticed that throughout history, it is through the awareness of individuals, who are living in a new spiritual consciousness, which transforms the universe. We begin by thinking and planning an idea in our mind, feel the desire to see our idea carried out, then we set about the task to create a piece of work to realise our ideas.

A true artist is a scientist, priest and philosopher who carry out on the physical plane that which intelligence conceives as truth and yet the creative work depends on the self-transcending power of his imagination. The source of creativity is biological since every artist has elements of an enquiring mind and through their work, no matter how diverse, teaches others about their perceptions of the world. Artists and scientists have a gift to be able to interpret an ordinary experience in the light of eternity and translate this perception into human terms, using a tangible image. This bridge between two planes of humanity and universal mystery can only be effective if interpreted within familiar objects. It is by living on both levels at once, that the scientist and artist can experience a brief look at nirvana.

The search for the transcendent experience is one of the most powerful instincts in the human psyche, which may lead to an inner transformative experience, where connection to the divine is perceived as being at one with the whole universe.

Throughout history, human knowledge and understanding have been reflected upon and translated into a variety of art forms. For example, the poets Blake, Wordsworth, Goethe, the photographer Blossfeldt and composer Stockhausen have all used the creative process to relate their personal perception of nature.

Globally, indigenous peoples have always viewed non-ordinary states of consciousness as an experimental connection to the cosmos, during which guidance is received.

Looking at a variety of cultural philosophies, it is apparent that there is a deep respect towards the spiritual in nature. Pantheism is an ancient religion that is older than Buddhism or Christianity. Most Taoist, many Chinese, Japanese, deep ecologists and followers of many native religions are Pantheists. These are disciples, who care for nature, admire and respect the universe and celebrate life and so I believe there is a deep-seated need within the human psyche to make this connection with nature, in order to ascertain an identity of our place within the universe. With the diminishing religious doctrines, nature appears to have become a source of divine inspiration for many artists. The spiritual interpretation is evident in the mountainous landscapes of Caspar Friedrich, (1774- 1840) whose paintings are greatly influenced by the spiritual in the Chinese landscape paintings, while the English artist

Joseph Turner's (1779-1851) awareness of nature's energy and power was very different. Through experiencing the full force of a violent storm at sea, by strapping himself to the mast of a ship, Turner was then able to interpret such power and spiritual presence of nature's forces within his paintings, as he used almost tactile communication to represent the energy of the storm. This overwhelming insight of grandeur and turbulence, typified in Turner's paintings, expresses man's emotions of being confronted and overpowered by natures forces.

There is a spiritual quality in Turner's work which is communicated to the onlooker. In particular, the light in the atmosphere, typical in many of his paintings, maybe interpreted as nature's energy and life source. Often, the artist leaves the observer to formulate their own concepts from the objects within the surface colour, each of which can be isolated from each other, only with great difficulty. Perhaps this device may have been used to suggest the vibration of natural forms with the source energy. There are total scenes of nature, trees, leaves, figures and clouds, all vibrating with bright source energy.

At the beginning of the Twentieth Century, with the advancement of science and Darwin's theory, that nature is constantly changing with man, as a result of evolution, there is now an understanding that we are in a state of flux rather than fixed creations. The Physicist Albert Einstein (1879-1955) supported this theory, by providing scientific evidence that all things are vibrating with energy and that matter was nothing more than a form of light.

'Things we perceive with our slowly vibrating senses are energies vibrating at the same slow rate. All things that vibrate, within what we call the physical range, appear to us to be solid matter. Science has shown that when any object is reduced down to its 'smallest particle', it is made up of millions of sparks of energy'.

Einstein's discoveries greatly contributed to this chronological shift, due to the realisation of not living in a solid mass, but in a universe full of intricate energy systems in dynamic fields of energy. However, there are similarities between this new physics and the Eastern philosophies of Hinduism, Buddhism and Taoism, a sort of interconnecting web of relationships.

The advancement of scientific knowledge is also reflected in the work of the Impressionist artist Claude Monet (1840-1926), who was aware of Turners captivating effects of light and atmospheric conditions that revealed more than the subject of the painting. Monet was more concerned in recording his own changing perceptions, rather than depicting the object. This is evident in the series of paintings of 'Rouen Cathedral'. The technique of applying small dabs of colour, gives the impression of vibrating energy and a mass of particles, rather than the solidity of masonry.

When talking about subject matter, Monet stated:

'The subject does not matter. One instant, one aspect of nature is all that is needed, since every aspect of nature will hold the life source.

Look at it (water) you thought of infinity; you are able to discern it, as in a microcosm, the presence of the elements and the instability of a Universe that changes constantly under our very eyes...Perhaps my originality boils down to being a hypersensitive receptor and to the expediency of shorthand which I project on a canvas, as if on a screen.'

There are so many paintings of Monet's 'Grain-stacks' with the obvious concern about space and time and yet there are also parallels to connect reality and a deep consciousness, as used in meditation to achieve a higher level of awareness. There is an almost celestial quality to his work.

The English critic, Brownell, was of the opinion that:

'Monet's art had become nature itself, with not a line anywhere, just the suggestion of form'

This idea correlates with the new scientific research of that time, suggesting objects are made up of clusters of life source energy. As science and technology advanced further into the Twentieth Century, referring to the theories of Quantum physics, Zukav states the possibility of being able to measure particles of light and also variance of light frequencies, proving that other forms of life co-exist but are invisible. He also supports the view that:

'The multi-sensory personality is more radiant and energetic than a five sensory personality because the person is aware of forms of life that are invisible to a five sensory personality.'

The British Biologist, Harry Oldfield, has now developed a method of photography which produces images of light energy, emanating from all living things. Oldfield has also experimented with various light frequencies, proving that other forms of life co-exist but are invisible.

The idea of a person's increased perceptions results in an awareness of the energy source found in all forms of life, corresponds with the idea of creative and sensitive artists, in the widest sense, are more likely to experience this phenomenon. For example, when the artist Therese Oulton creates paintings and mono-prints, she establishes a process to include alchemy within her art in her attempt to 'turn painterly mud into light'. There are frequent references to this methodology when Oulton makes a visual connection of rock with gold, as riches hidden in the core of the earth, with the duality of relating the soul within, each inseparable from the other. She recalls in 'Cast' that fossils deep in the earth contain and emit their own light. This is further evidence that Oulton includes matter and the spiritual within her work about nature.

From a different perspective, the artist Anish Kapoor attains a fundamental spiritual dimension within his drawings, sculpture and prints. He experiments with a variety of techniques to create form without drawing, by eradicating line. (Monet also painted without line). This results in an image that appears to be floating.

In order to achieve an art that is both of the human and spiritual experience, Kapoor combines the Western tradition of Turner, mysticism of Blake, together with the spiritual from his Indian culture. It is for wholeness that Kapoor is searching in his work, a connectedness with the universe, believing that the smallest motifs have a great presence.

In the manner of Monet and Oulton, Kapoor's mark making are made instinctively, whereby the artist acts as a communicator of forces and meditations beyond the conscious. This same observation was made of Monet when reading extracts from his letters referring to his methodologies:

> 'The only virtue in me is my submission to instinct; it is because I rediscovered and allowed intuitive and secret forces to predominate that I was able to identify with creation and become absorbed by it. My art is an act of faith, an act of love and humility.... I applied paint to these canvases in the same way as monks of old illuminated their books of hours; they owe everything to the close union of solitude and silence, to a passionate and exclusive attention akin to hypnosis'.

Oulton too refers to experiencing this transcendental state when talking about her prints:

> 'They seem to belong to another culture-given the frail paper, the woodcut quality, their remoteness-even though they are refutably from my hand'.

On his observations of Kapoor's methodologies, Jeremy Lewison, formerly Director of the Tate Gallery, stated:

'Each drawing is usually begun near the centre of the sheet and while it develops relatively spontaneously Kapoor knows from the outset what kind of motif he is dealing with. Many of these marks are made instinctively, the artist acting as a transmitter of forces and thoughts beyond the conscious'.

It is very important to me to interpret the spiritual in nature, from my perspective and I hope to achieve this through morphology. I too, am fascinated with alchemy, in the way substances react with each other, making my own tools to obtain different mark making and with an interest in the science of particle physics. I have contacted physicists who specialise in this field, in order to gain knowledge to enable me to achieve my aims.

Since the beginning of time, man has acknowledged the spiritual in nature, as shown in the various cultural philosophies. It is evident that work produced by each generation is the recognition that the hidden creative forces triumph everywhere. The unification of the Eastern harmony with the universal flow, combined with the Western ability to transform new data, is a significant shift towards wholeness of humanity that is fundamental to our emerging spirituality. Together, the harmony and action take us to new levels of evolution but the advancement of this structure dependent on the joint collaboration and pooling of resources to form the whole.

The enormous shift in the Twenty-First Century is that human evolution will occur consciously. According to the author James Redfield, we will learn new ways of being, connecting to universal thought through intuition and being guided to live from a place of creativity, rather than from a position of control. There is a human need to make a connection with natural forces to ascertain an identity of our place within nature. Through creativity, the human can relate to this experience.

Chapter 3

Ancient Wisdoms

I wish to make a deeper connection to others throughout my life and work and so this radiates out a level of support that assists the growth of new thinking. Our radiating thoughts and feelings cause our energy to flow out into the world and affect other energy systems.

I would like to share with you a few examples of the Shamanic wisdoms from a wide variety of cultures, which I have found both interesting and inspirational:

'Listen! Or your tongue will make you deaf.'   Cherokee saying.

'We are all flowers in the Great Spirits garden. We share a common root and the root is Mother Earth. The garden is beautiful because it has different colours in it and those colours represent different traditions and cultural backgrounds.'   Grandfather David Mongye (Hopi).

'All life is Waken, so also is everything which exhibits power, whether in action, as the winds and drifting clouds, or in the wayside for even the commonest sticks and stones have a spiritual essence which must be revered as a manifestation of the all-pervading mysterious power that fills the Universe.'   Francis Laflesche/ Osage (North American Indian).

'All things are in the Universe, and the Universe is in all things, we in it, and it in us, and in this way, everything harmonises in perfect unity.'

Giordano Bruno-Pantheist martyr.

In the book, 'Earth Medicine', by Kenneth Meadow, there is a beautiful, perceptive poem called, 'The Spirit of the Redman':

'I am with you now.
In the ever-changing Present
That is true Eternity
Closer than the breath
That brings your body life.
Closer than the thought
That springs within the mind
That ignorant men call finite.
Closer than the beat
That keeps your heart in tune.
For I am to be found Nowhere
But where you are.
For I am the One that is All
And can be seen in all.
Anywhere.
Everywhere

Chapter 4
The Importance of Communicating the Visual Image

In order to communicate through the art images, the sublime messages need to be interpreted by the onlooker. I try not to discuss my work in depth for this very reason. I wish the onlooker to think and interpret the messages for themselves. If this doesn't happen, then it is my job to reinvent a way to communicate more clearly.

The artist should be aware of the important task they should be developing in the remodelling of the human race, after learning the laws of spiritual, physical and divine, to encourage them to find a world of beauty and wonder for themselves, vibrating on a higher plane of soul and spirit.

Throughout the history of our planet, it is not only the evolution of technology, but also the evolution of thought, that are the building blocks of man's understanding of his environment. Physicists are now pursuing the bewildering process fundamental to human life with 'The Theory of Everything'.

It is important for scientists to become involved in this research so they are able to provide scientific facts in order to allay scepticism while helping us understand the nature of the universe. Everything occurs in nature following some natural law. Through the work of Albert Einstein, we now understand that there is an energy travelling through all matter which was previously perceived as solid form, including ourselves. Matter is only energy vibrating at certain frequencies, even in its simplest form. Animals absorb organic life in order to sustain their energy vibration.

Chapter 5

Energy Emitting from Nature

On my Masters course, I was able to explore the idea of energies in nature even further, incorporating Albert Einstein's 'Theory of Everything' within my work, his idea of $E=MC2$, showing that there was no such thing as solid matter, but all things were made up of pure light energy. I understood from my teaching, that various cultures acknowledge this universal energy, having different names such as the Asian Prana, in China it is referred to as Chi, or Ki in Japan, all of which I incorporated within my work, with the aim of communicating my ideas across various cultures.

This clusters of energy emanates in nature, through humans too and actually surrounds us by way of auras. When healing with Reiki, meditating or using various Eastern traditions, often the practitioner or Shaman work with those auras, some being various colours, encircling the form, which denote the health and wellbeing of the patient.

Chapter 6

Methodologies

Being concerned with the mystery and reality of what makes us who we are and to achieve an understanding of our universe, I believe that art may be used as a vehicle to contribute to a deeper appreciation of our existence. This profound curiosity about the functioning of our universe, has led me, as an artist, on a never-ending quest to find a language to interpret my experience of our world.

It has been through working in the landscape that my perceptions have developed and I now realise that all of nature has the same life source energy, the elements, flora and fauna too.

Through research and constant experimentation, I try to physically translate a concept with a message, into each piece of work, in a coherent way. It is very important to me to communicate this information in an endeavour to promote an understanding of our universe and to help preserve the very nature which sustains our planet. My personal way of seeing corresponds with the intellectual phenomenon of particle physics, a science that defines the realities of our world whereby fundamental particles and forces hold together all matter in our universe. I have a vision to communicate this essence of life within my work.

Regular exposure to this natural environment feeds and attunes a variety of senses such as sound, smell, touch and the visual, contributing to the whole experience of the celebration of nature. As a result of this interaction with nature, my perceptions have developed even further, in my endeavour to communicate this source energy within various media of my artwork.

I am aware that in nature, there are no edges and no solidity. Every small particle is a cluster of energy, all vibrating in an immense void. There are infinite fields of energy, all vibrating at different frequencies, ever flowing, ever changing, renewing and in a state of transformation. I feel each of us is connected by this energy source, including our environment and that every form is essentially energy, all vibrating and in transition.

When I am forming a piece of work, I try to stay focused on my aim, even though I am not quite sure of the outcome. I am aware that this is a common statement adopted by other artists. For example, the artists Kapoor, Picasso and Francis Bacon adopt this common ground and yet, from a personal perspective, I am on a journey of discovery and with each piece of work, I strive to take a step forward. Unfortunately, this is often not the case but it is only through a constant process of experimentation, with a variety of media, mark making, colour, scale etc. followed by an evaluation, development, modification and refining of my work, that I hope to realise my intentions with purpose and meaning.

As nature is my inspiration, I frequently walk in the forests, open countryside, rural and coastal paths, collecting stones, shells, leaves, tree bark and other items from the environment to use as a resource for my work. I may use the found objects in a variety of ways. For example, small studies of light or weather conditions have been used for reference for a painting within the studio, leaves and tree bark resources have also been used as inspiration within the studio landscape paintings. Impressions of leaves have been used to vary the mark-making, while the wood found in situ has been used to make tools to extend my repertoire of varying mark-making during the print process.

Looking for sources of new imagery, I return to nature, where there is a vast amount of data which I have yet to explore. With flora, fauna, a variety of seasons, atmospheric condition, the elements of wind, water, earth, strata of rock formations, caves, sea etc, this 'new' imagery is endless. For example, from a small watercolour study painted from direct observation within the forest, (see fig 9),

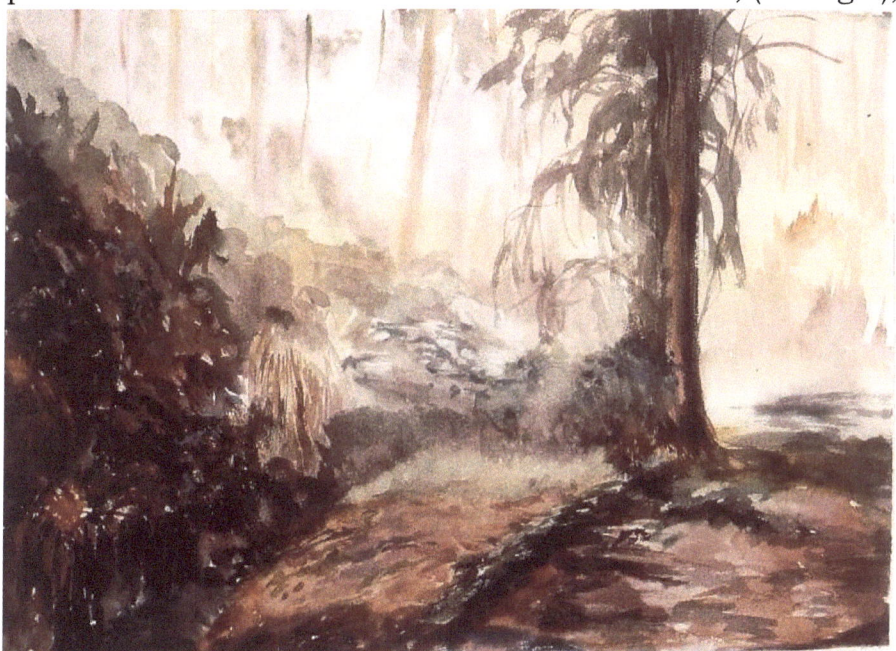

Fig 9 Watercolour.

I explored a variety of mark making within the studio using mono-type printing and coloured inks, (see fig 10),

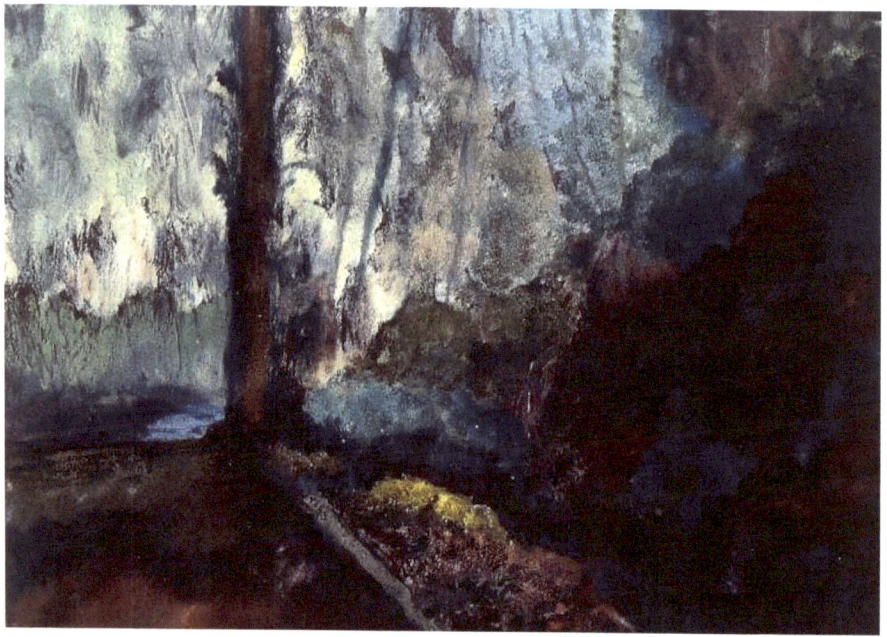

Fig 10 Mono-type & coloured inks.

mono-print and pastels, (see fig 11, fig 12),

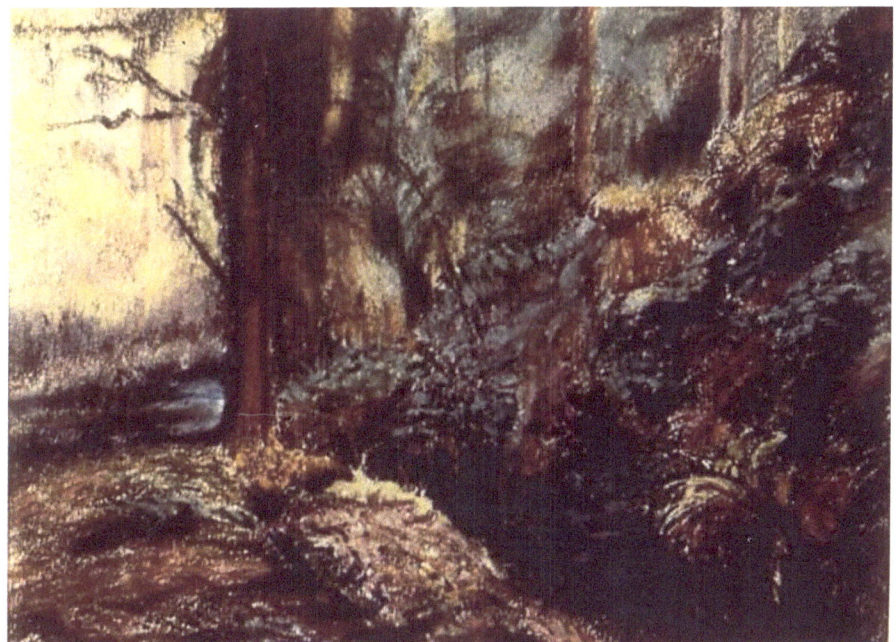

Fig 11 Mono-type & Pastels.

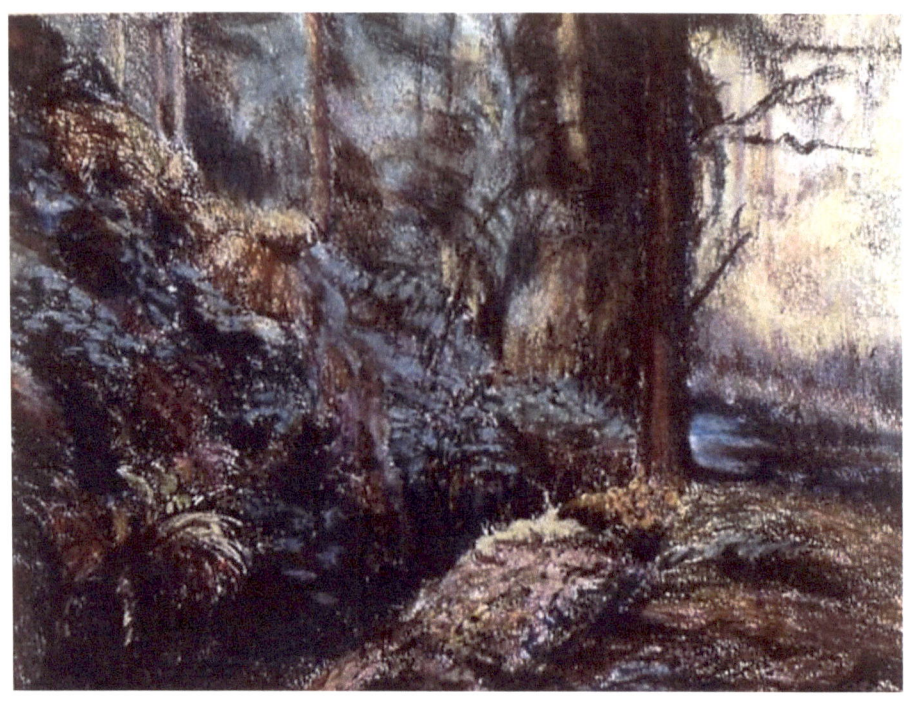

Fig 12 Mono-type & pastels.

mono-print from my Log book (see figs 13,14 &15) and developing into a final oil painting on board using red ground. (See fig16).

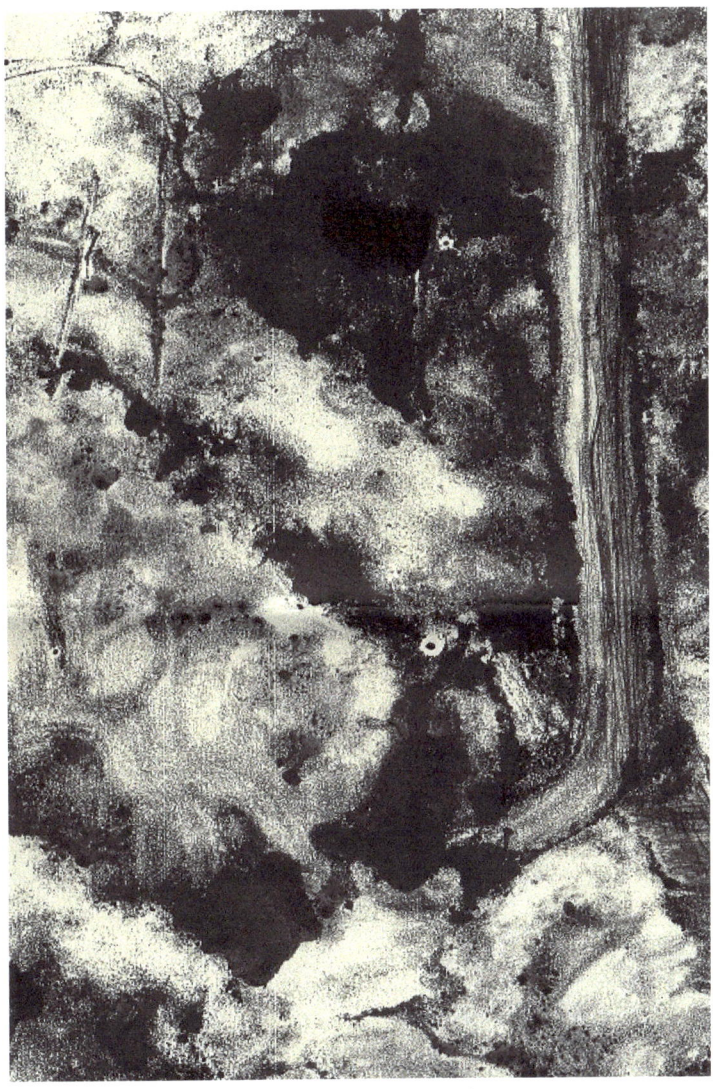

Fig 13 Mono-print.

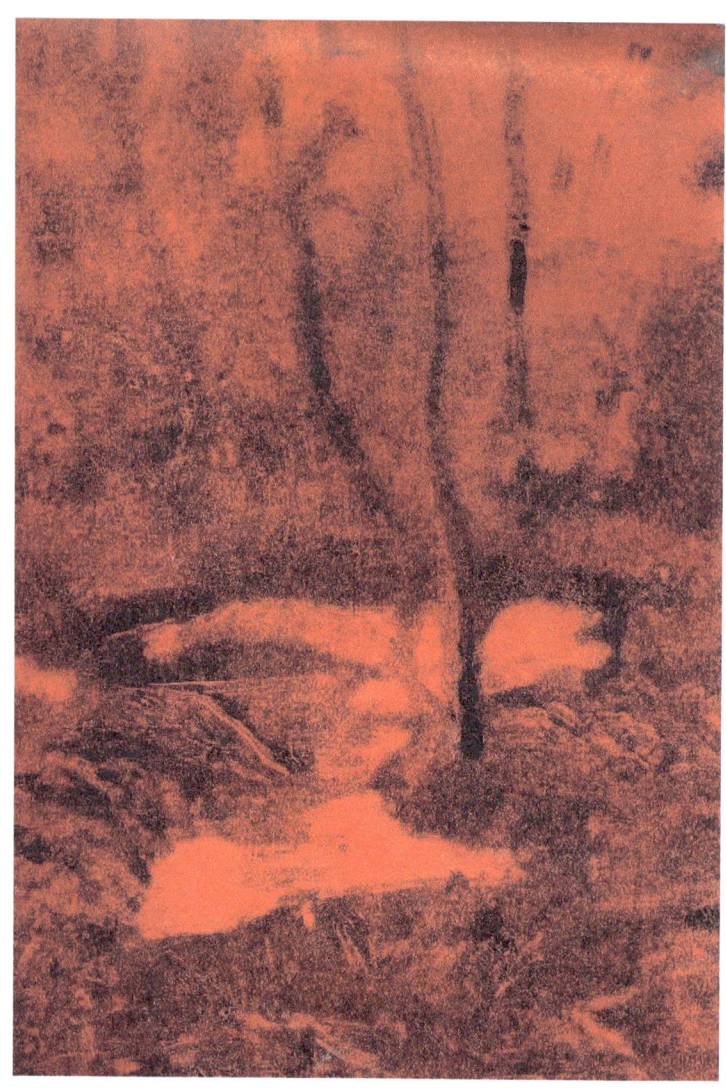

Fig 14 Mono-print.

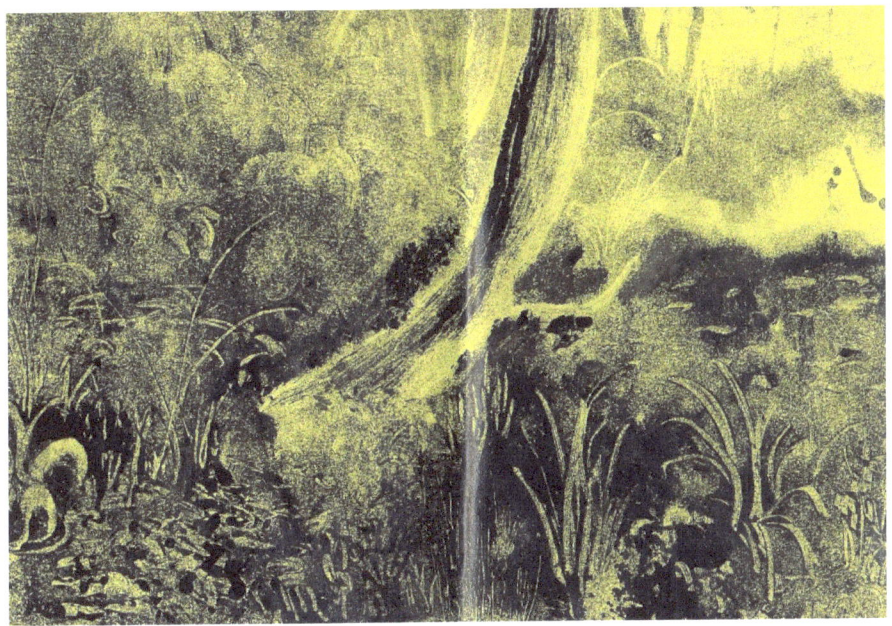

Fig 15 Mono-print.

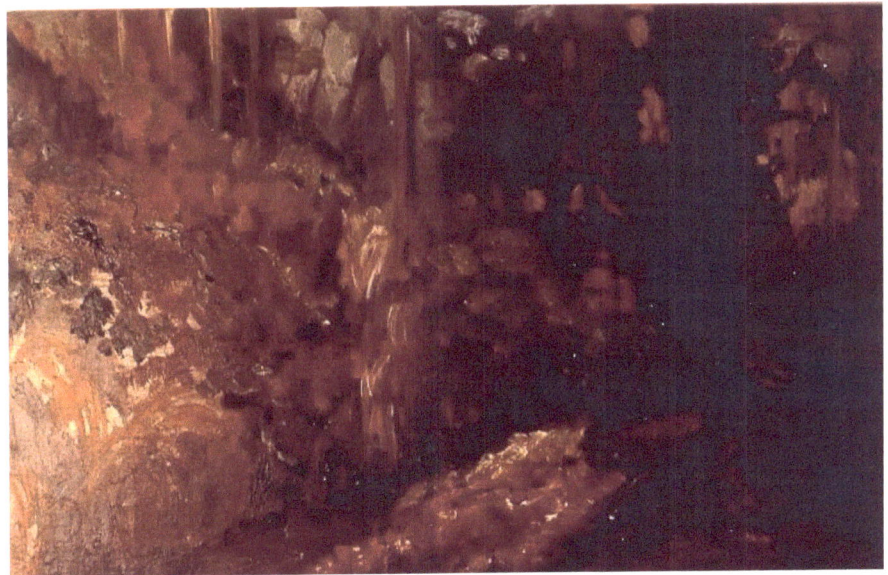

Fig 16 Oil painting on board.

I realise that any particular way of looking at a problem is only one way among many other possible solutions. I am constantly looking for a different approach to correspond with my ideas and translate them into a physical outcome. I have overlaid various print techniques, combined with mixed media over mono-prints, experimented with a whole host of substances in an endeavour to produce something new, different, while obtaining the desired effect.

Recently, I have tried to simplify my task by taking one specific specimen of either a plant or a flower, in order to work in isolation. Only then have I realised that the isolated subject contains within itself, the same complexities of energy of the whole forest landscape.

During my time in the forest environment, I became aware of secluded areas between the trees, almost like unique, magical glades, emitting vibrating energy, with the vertical of the trees providing screens to maintain privacy. (See fig17. Monoprint).

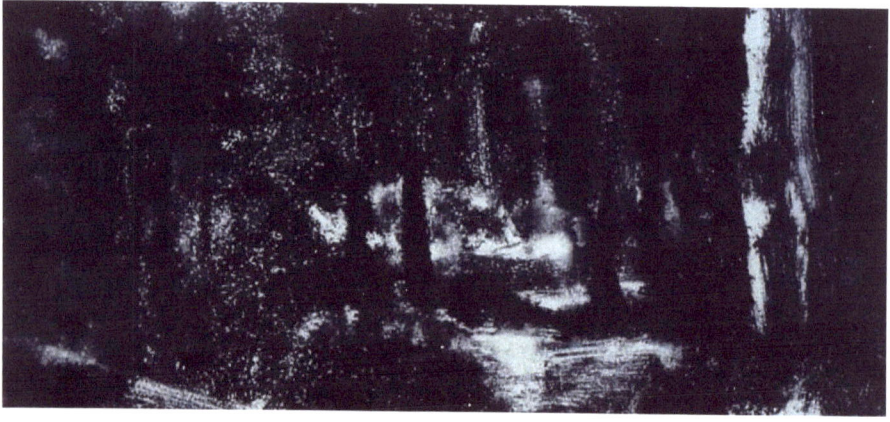

Fig 17 Mono-print.

Only then, did I discover the work of the artist Ivan Hitchens, (1893-1979), whose woodland paintings portrayed the verticals of the trees, divided up into separated areas within the forest interior. I know too, I have been greatly influenced by Monet's' paintings, with the way he interprets the essence of nature and being able to identify with much of his philosophies too. In Monet's painting, it is obvious that his use of small dabs of colour suggest a vibrating sensation, one I hoped to achieve within my work. (See fig 18. Oil on Board).

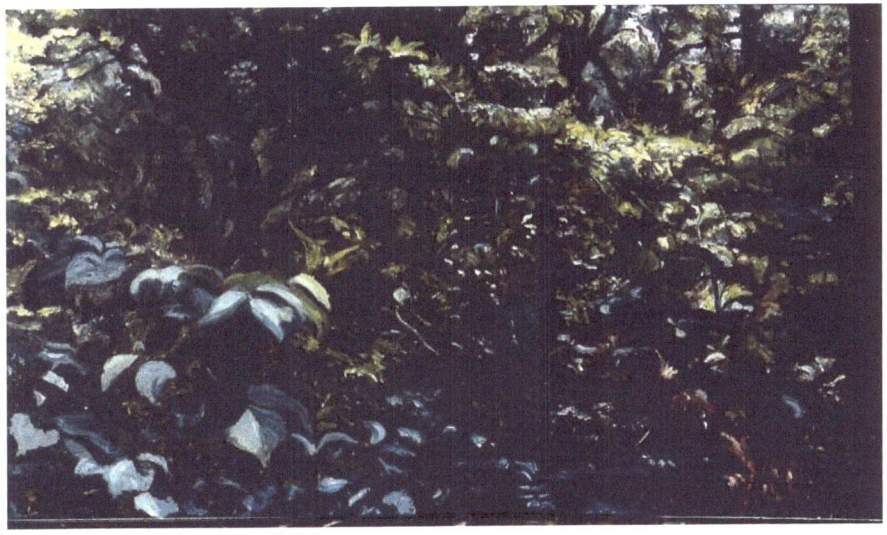

Fig 18 'Spring'. Oil painting on board.

There is also the colour palette of the artist David Bomberg, (1890-1957), using lots of pinks, purples, and blues to represent earth colours, most evident in my early landscapes. (See figs 19 & 20. Oil on board and canvas).

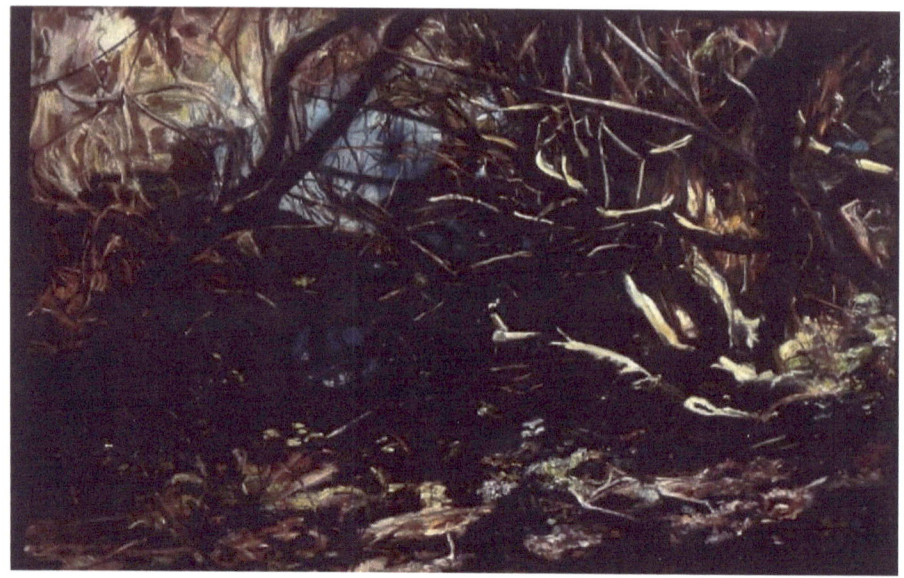

Fig 19 'New Beginnings.' Oil on canvas.

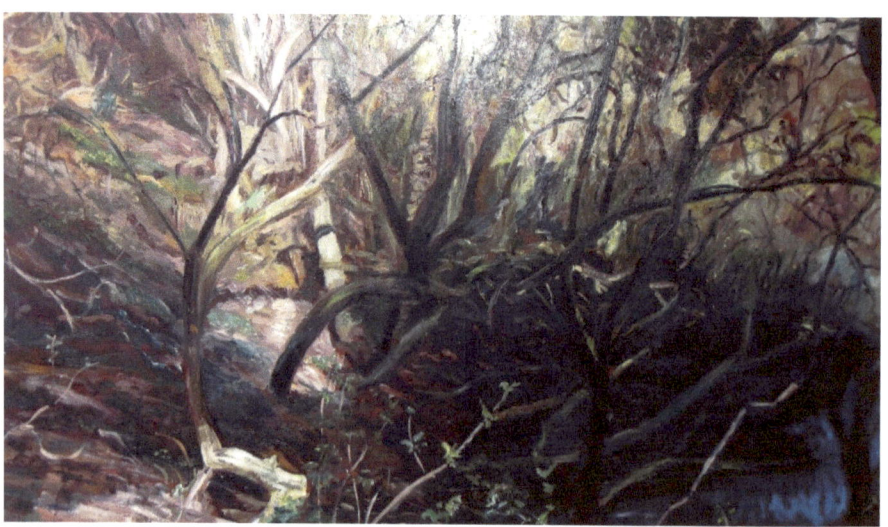

Fig 20 'Thicket' No2 Oil on board.

I had not noticed those similarities until it was pointed out to me by one of the University tutors.

There were a series of large floral coloured mono-prints which followed, altering the scale of the floral images, due to the inspiration by the artist Georgia O'Keefe, (1887-1986), when I was still concentrating on isolating a subject, which contained within itself, the same complexities of energies as the whole forest landscape. (See oil painting on board, fig 21, mono-print fig22).

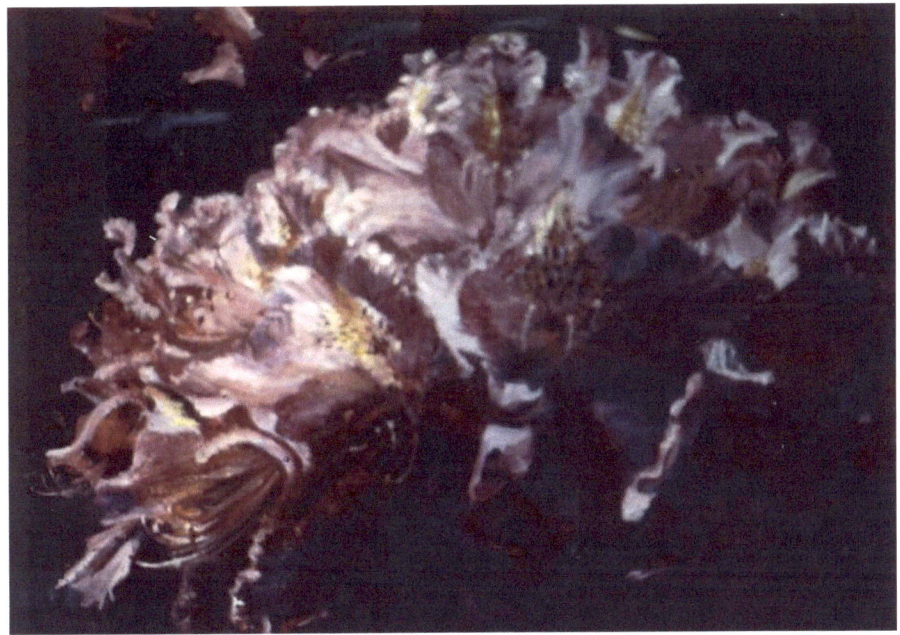

Fig 21 'Poetic Gradations' Oil on board.

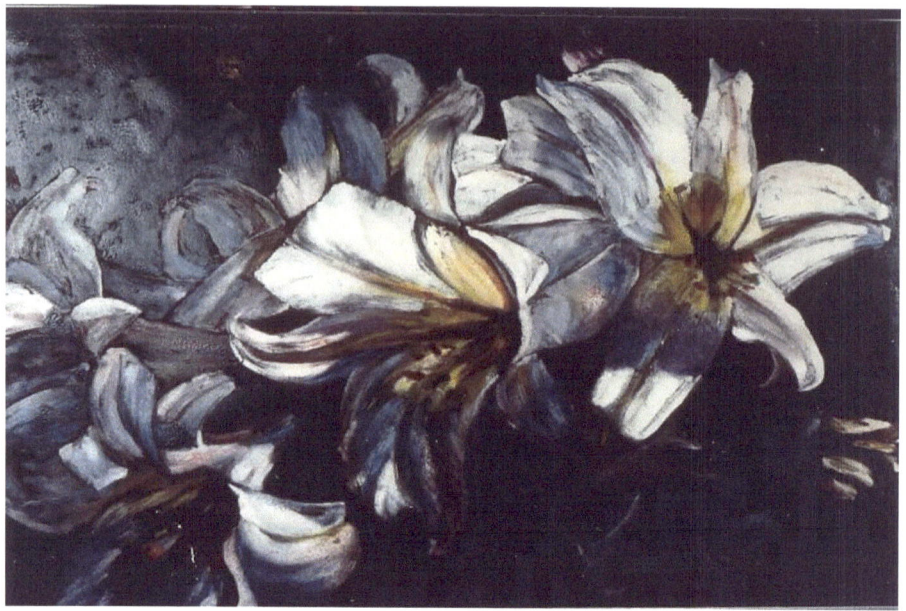

Fig 22 'Lilies' Mono-print.

It was way back in the early 1980's when I first became aware of the great power of nature's energy when painting the turbulent sea near cliff tops in Pembrokeshire, Wales. (See figs 23,24 & 25. Oil paintings on canvas).

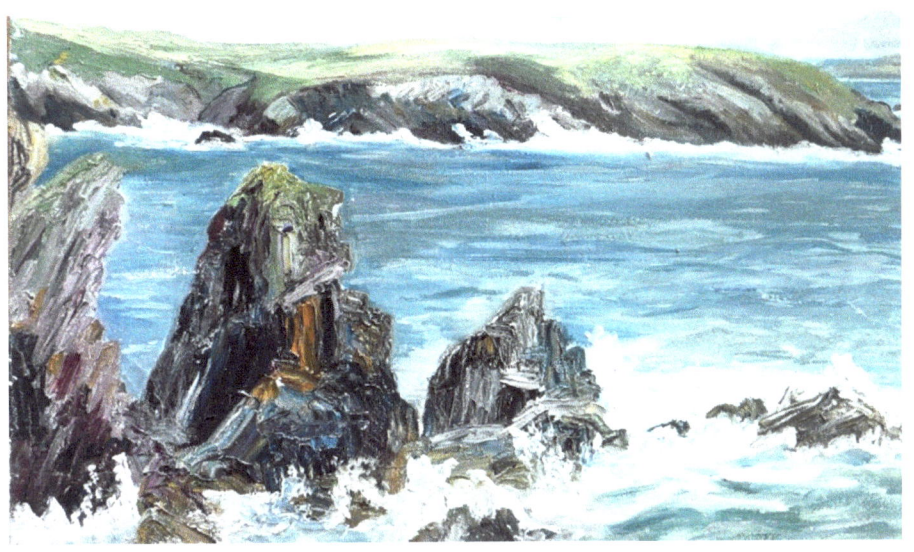

Fig 23 Pembrokeshire, Wales. Oil painting.

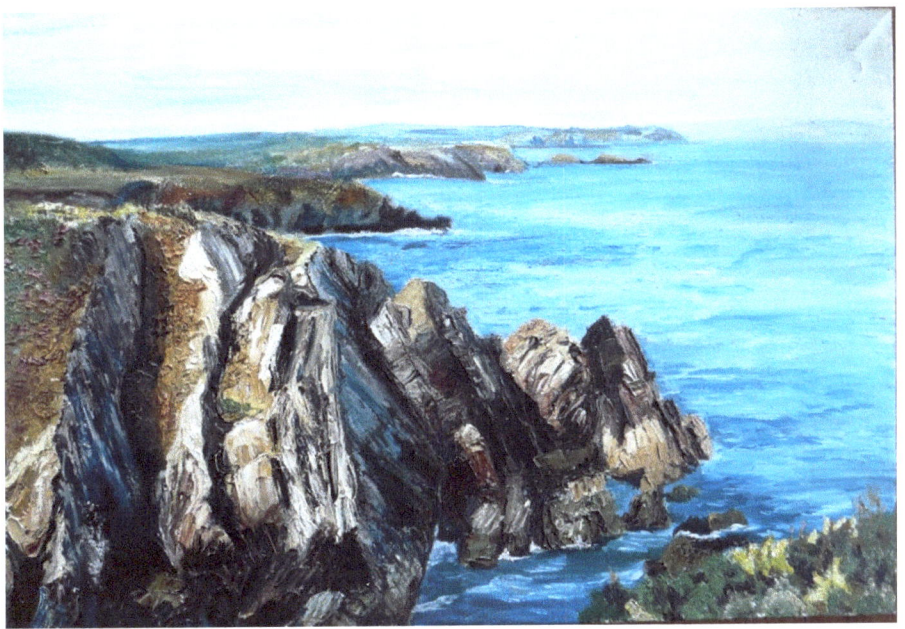

Fig 24 Pembrokeshire, Wales. Oil painting.

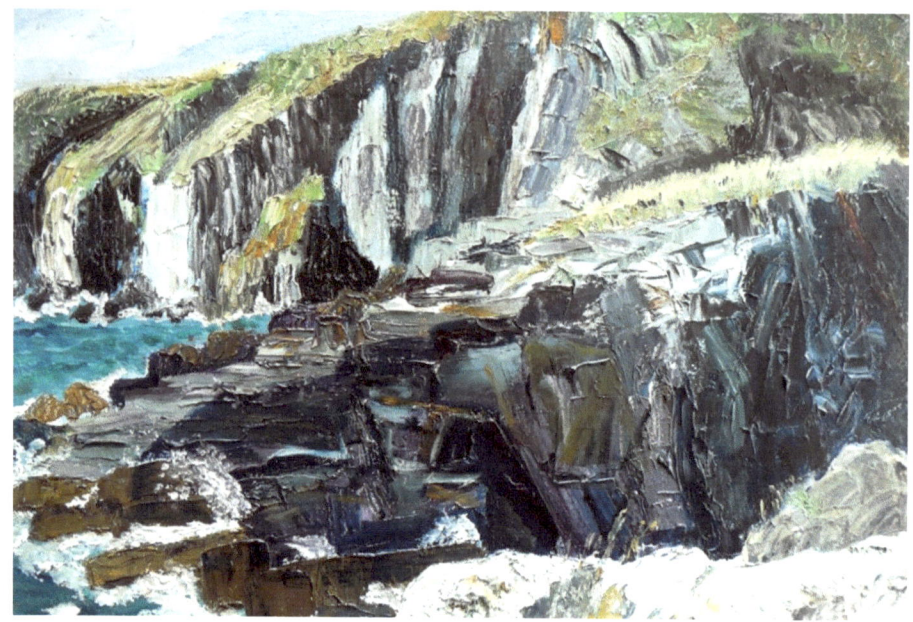

Fig 25 Pembrokeshire, Wales. Oil painting.

During my research, I noticed that in Monet's early career, he too painted dramatic seascapes before progressing to simplifying the landscape, by using the subject in isolation. However, I feel drawn towards the scientific identity of morphology with atoms emanating energy, with a continuous drive towards 'simplification', although I suspect there is no such state.

I share some common aims with Kapoor. Radiance is of central importance to our work; an interest in the mysteries of alchemy in the endless pursuit of the ultimate aim and our work is the expression of the quest to approach nearer to the truth. I am extremely interested in the evolution of my artwork and the development of self.

Chapter 7

Continuing with the Artistic Quest

I have a profound curiosity about the functioning of our universe and as an artist, I am on a never-ending journey to find a language to interpret my experience of our world. Through research and constant experimentation, I try to physically translate a concept, together with a sublime message into each piece of work, in a coherent way. It is important to me to communicate this information in an endeavour to promote an understanding of our universe and to help preserve the very nature that sustains our planet.

I have focused on the forest interior as my primary source material for my work, looking at the flora, fauna, scientific data, together with the Eastern and Western philosophies, regarding energy in nature. I have explored areas of energy auras surrounding organic forms; (See Fig 26. Cyanotype print):

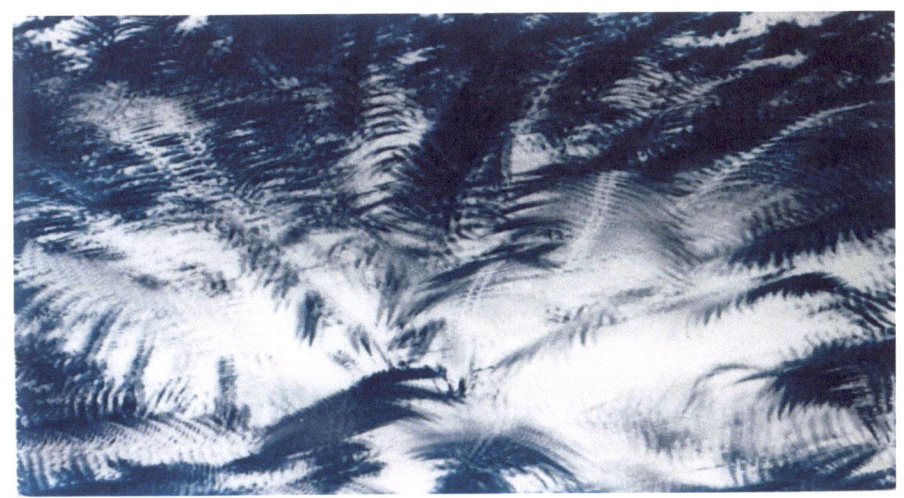

Fig 26 'Prana.' Cyanotype print.

I used digital texture mapping to fragment forms found in the forest interior to simulate vibrating energy;(See Fig 27. Screen print):

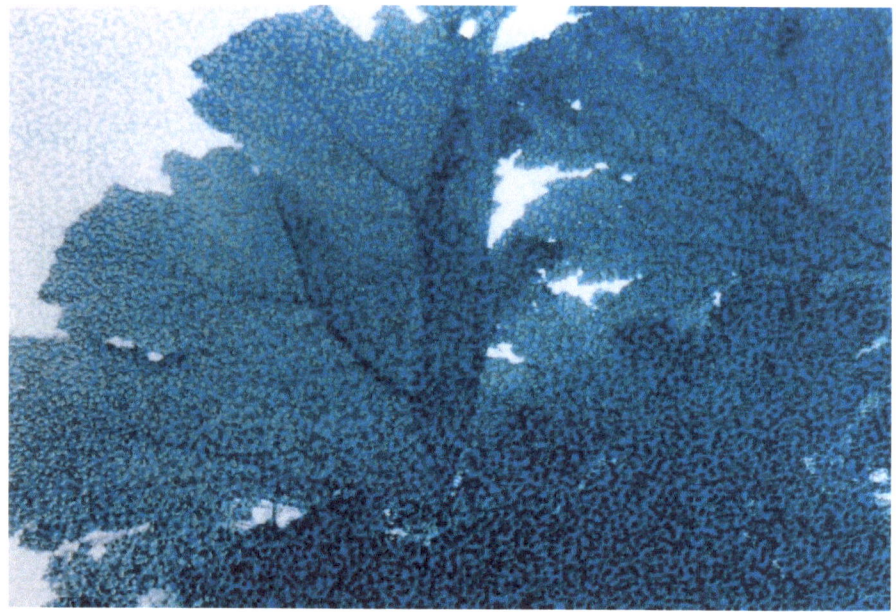

Fig 27 'Chi, The First Source.' Screen print.

I have produced twenty-eight-silk screens of multiple images, in an attempt to describe variations of Chi energy found in the forest. (See figs 28,29,30 & 31)

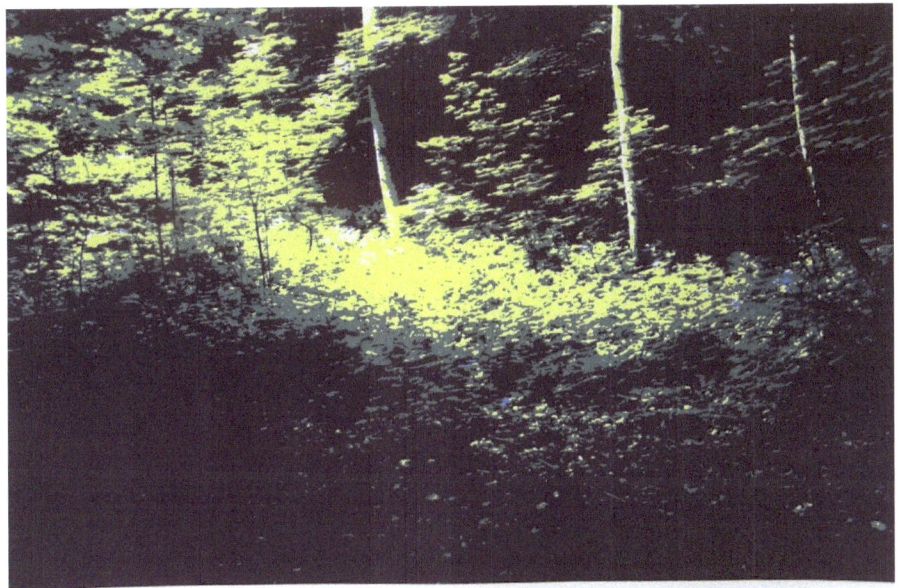

Fig 28 'Opening to the Knowledge' Screen print.

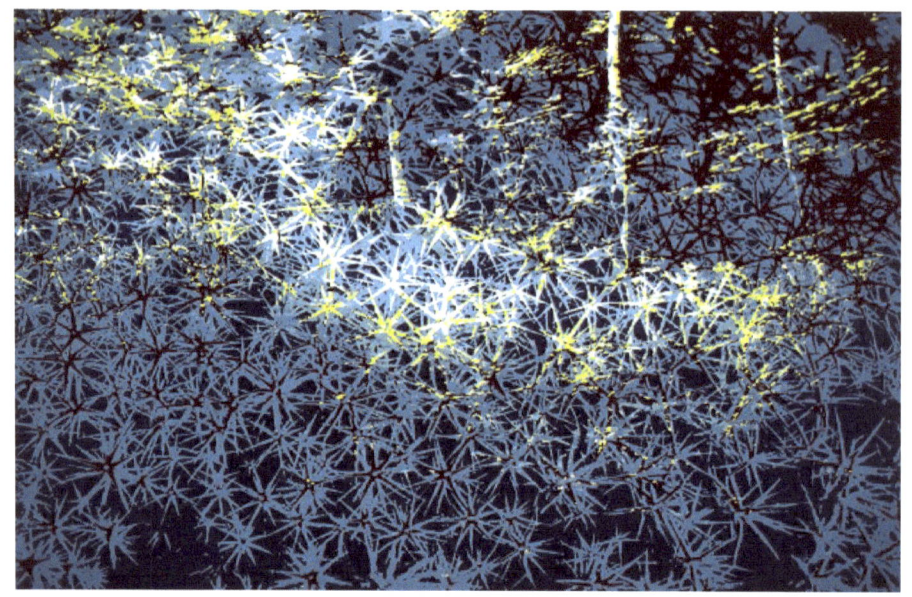

Fig 29 'Forest Chi.' No1. Screen print.

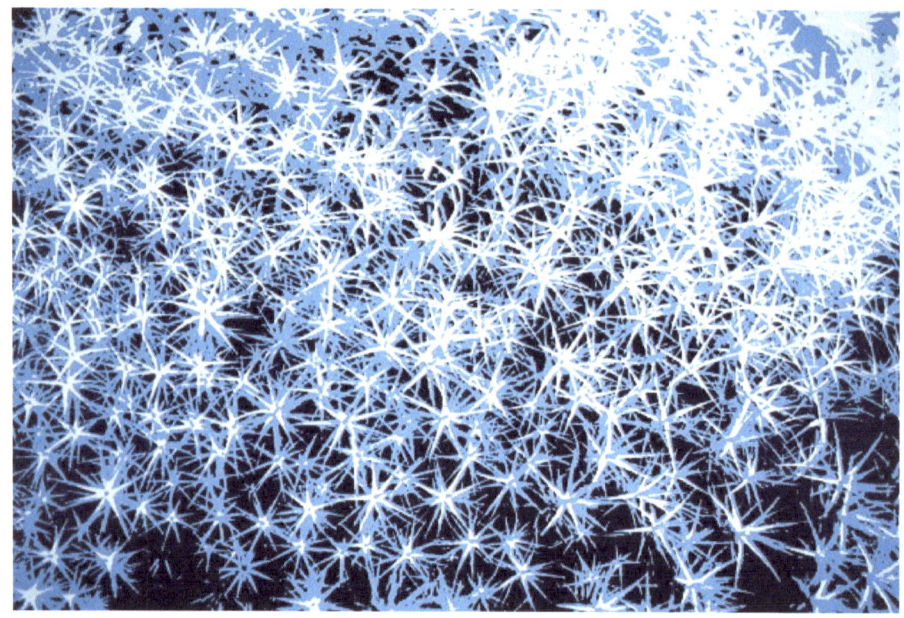

Fig 30 'Lichen' No3. Screen print.

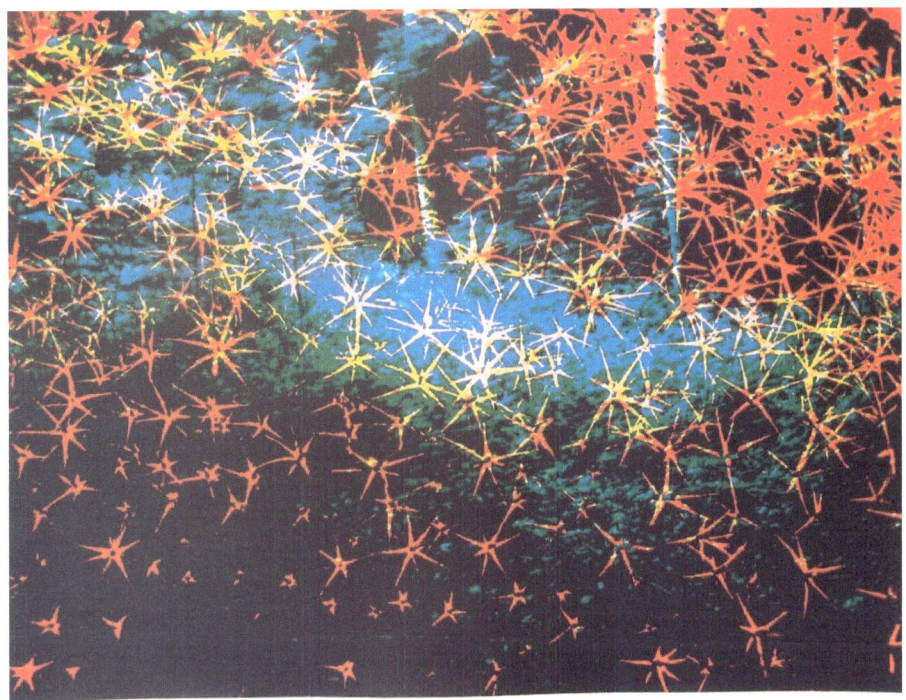

Fig 31 'Forest Chi.' No 29. Screen print.

Through a constant process of evaluation, development and refining of my work and ideas, my aim evolved to exhibit a series of projects, each displaying some aspect of the main theme to my work, i.e. the energy in nature.

During my time at University, studying for my Master's Degree, I ventured into a completely new arena for me, that of film making using digital imagery. I filmed the forest interior using both video and cine cameras.

I was very impressed with the flexibility of film making, with such massive potential for experimentation, particularly with special effects. With my increased confidence working in digital media, I embarked on producing a few films.

My first forest film incorporated special effects to suggest the vibrating tree energy, birdsong, rhythmic sound of the wind and also inserted script from ancient wisdoms, cultures and philosophies. (See fig 32 film clip).

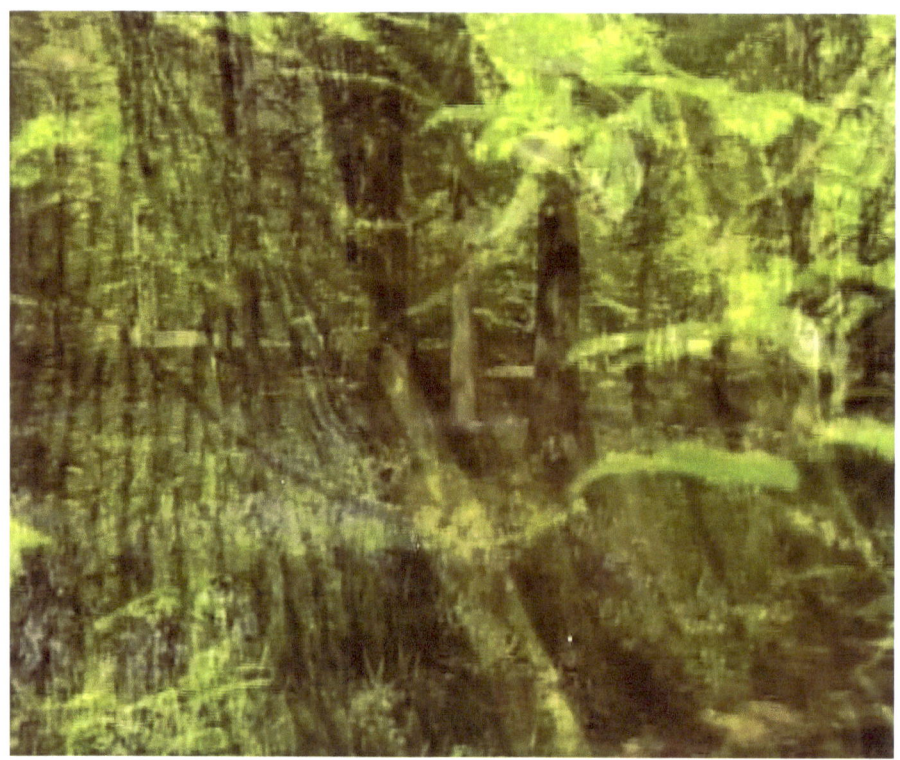

Fig 32 'Awakening.' Film Clip.

My next venture was to make a film that would show the slow, continuous change in nature, together with the ever-present energy. ('Forever Changing, in a State of Flux'). In order to obtain this effect, I made a large teleidoscope, then filmed the forest through the lens, the result being the whole forest environment slowly merges together, in a continuous, ever changing variety of shapes.

Since I was trying to simulate the whole forest interior within my Masters Exhibition, none of my work was to be viewed in isolation, but more of a immersion of a healing experience.

A further piece of work consisted of three pieces of screen-printed glass, each suspended in close proximity to each other. The observer would be invited to walk around the piece, endorsing the idea of the solidity of form is not always as it appears. The motif appears solid only when viewed from a central position. (See fig 33. Screen print on glass x 3)

Fig 33 'E=MC2.'   Screen print on glass.

After researching the work of James Lovelock, the scientist and environmentalist, I became fascinated in his ' Gaia Theory' where he proposes that the Earth functions as a self-regulating system. I then produced an animation from one of my watercolour paintings, to suggest a breathing planet, as my interpretation of Lovelock's 'Gaia Theory'. (See fig 34. Animation).

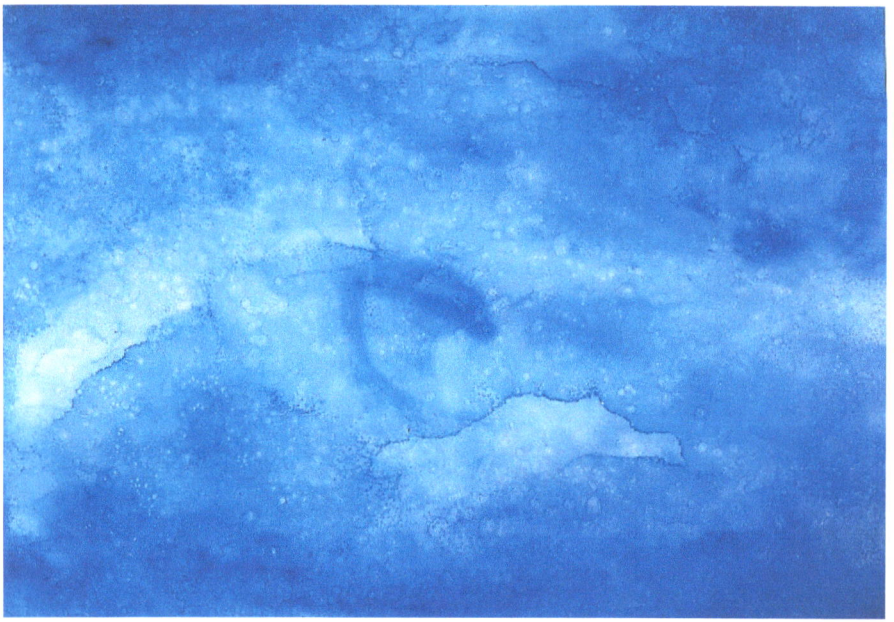

Fig 34 'Gaia Theory.' Animation.

Another glass piece of work in my exhibition, 'A New Dawn' was a further attempt to represent the forest interior. I screen printed the script, 'The Theory of Everything' on top of the glazed area of forest undergrowth, the filigree ferns and foliage created a very busy image which relates to the forest interior, to represent the current scientific research by physicists in their pursuit to analyse the energy found in all aspects of nature.

The script was purposely non-intrusive, using a similar colour palette, enhanced by strategically placed lighting, together with a water installation, serving as a small waterfall, found in the forest. Rocks and plants were also incorporated in the work so as to introduce not only the visual but also the additional sense of sound, with the introduction of water and birdsong. (See fig 35 & 36. Screen print on glass).

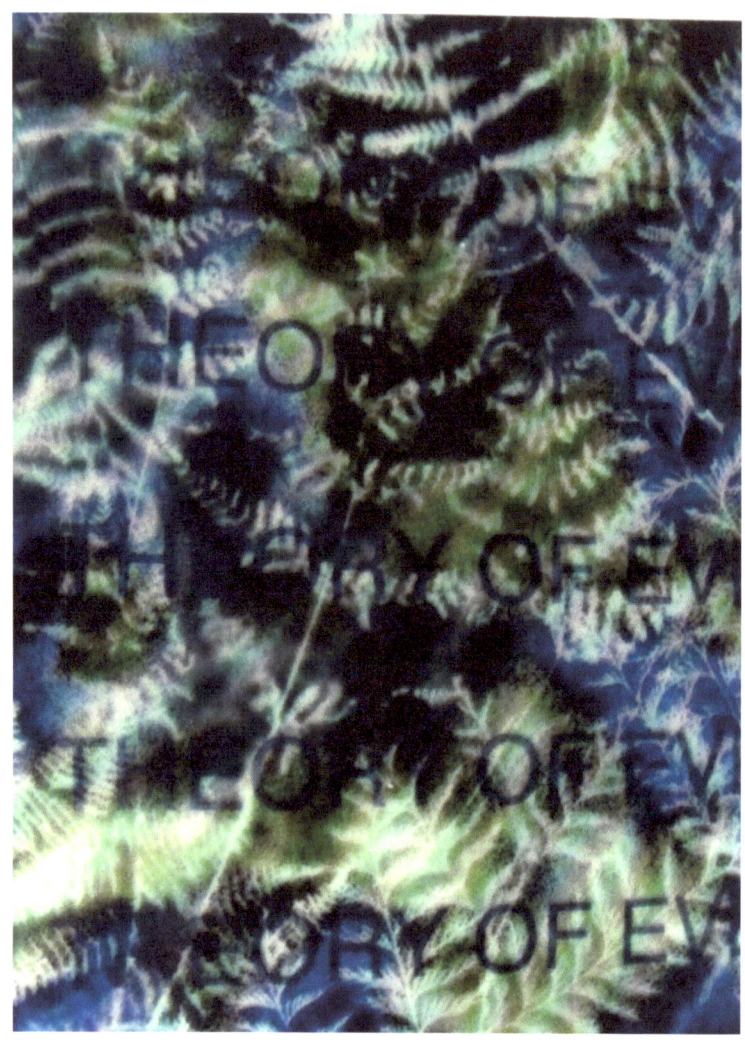

Fig 35 'A New Dawn.' Screen print on glass.

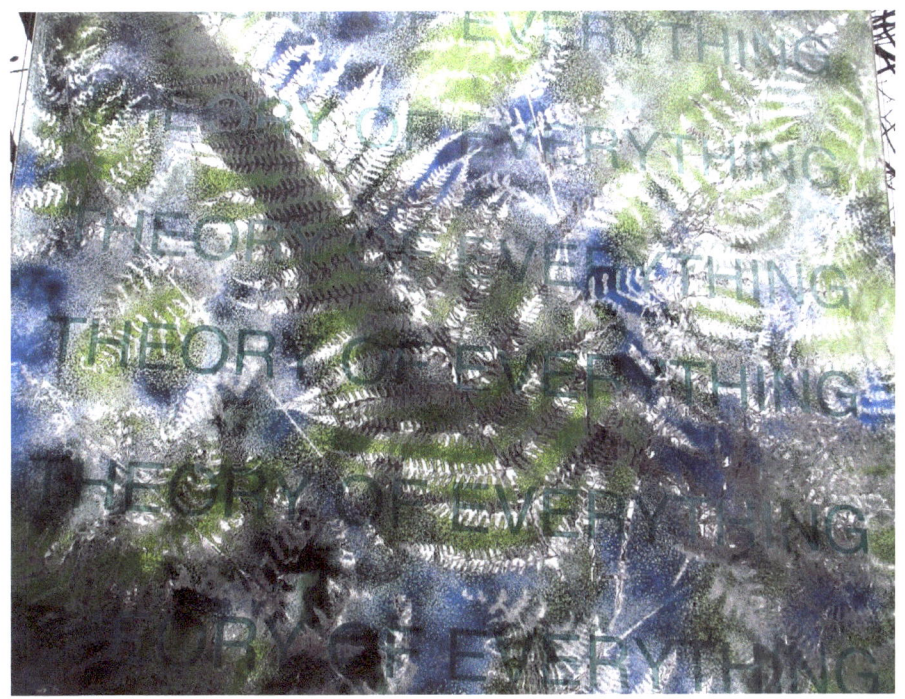

Fig 36 Glass in Romsey Botanical Gardens.

The incorporation of the script, 'The Theory of Everything' was fundamental in suggesting that all elements of nature hold this same source energy. This piece of work was later exhibited within the woodlands of Romsey Botanical Gardens, being suspended from a tree. Within this natural environment it sat well, almost being camouflaged, except for the sublime message it portrayed. (See fig 37. Section of screen print on glass).

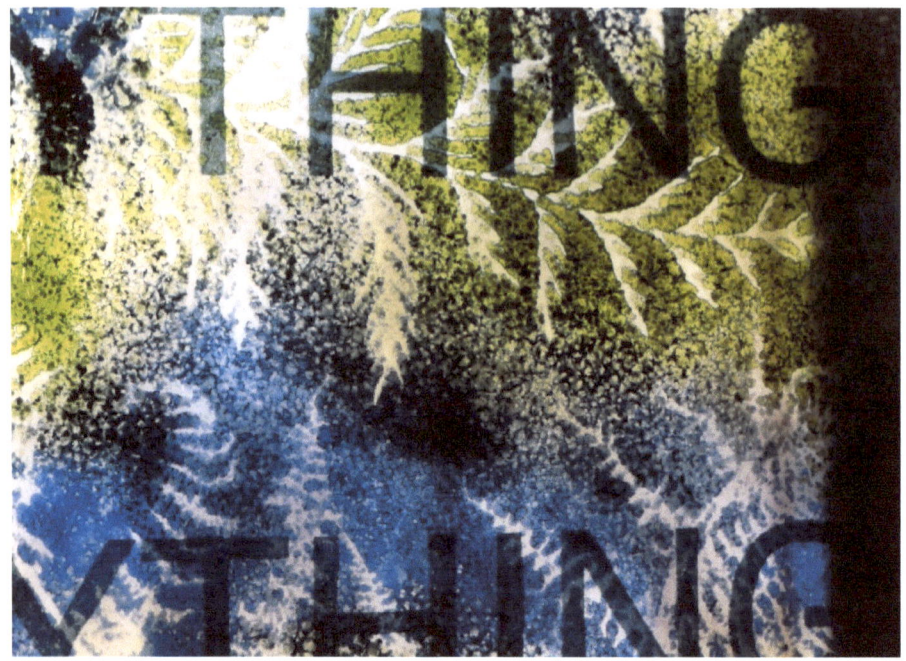

Fig 37 Section of 'A New Dawn.'   Screen print on glass.

Contemporary science is confirming that the material appearance of nature is an illusion and I believe that art is not only of aesthetic value but also comments on the realities that surround us. Studying a variety of cultural philosophies, I believe there is a deep-seated need within the human psyche to make connection with the spirit of nature, in order to ascertain an identity of our place within the universe.

Throughout my Exhibition, I made the conscious decision to use high vibration colours of light blues, turquoise and sea greens, with my work not to be seen in isolation, but as each piece containing a clue to the overall concept. I believe it is only through education and knowledge that people begin to understand the importance of how we are each interconnected by the source energy and the reliance of our survival on our living planet.

It was interesting to note how different a cross-section of society responded to my work since I tried to incorporate various nuances which corresponded to the life force radiating from the body, being recognised by many cultures. For example, the Native American Iroquois refer to this force as 'Orenda', India calls it 'Prana', Hebrew relate to 'Ruach', Polynesian Hunas refers to 'Mana', China refers to 'Chi', Japan refers to 'Ki', while Islam refers to 'Baraka'.

Some Chinese students commented about one of my films in the Exhibition and its Taoist content and how they were able to relate to the theme of the show, even sharing the additional Taoist proverb, 'You can never put your feet into the river in the same place twice'. Other members of the public visited on a daily basis to relax and meditate, some for at least one hour, sitting in silence and contemplating. Playing on the senses of audio, smell, together with the visual, my intention was to enhance the forest interior experience with running water, sounds of birdsong, wind rustling in the trees. Even natural plants and ferns were planted around the water's edge, together with films, prints, glass installation and animation, all containing sublime messages. Those messages were not only in the titles, but also in each piece of work, all in an effort to contribute to the healing natural environment of the forest. (See figs 38, 39 & 40. Viscosity prints).

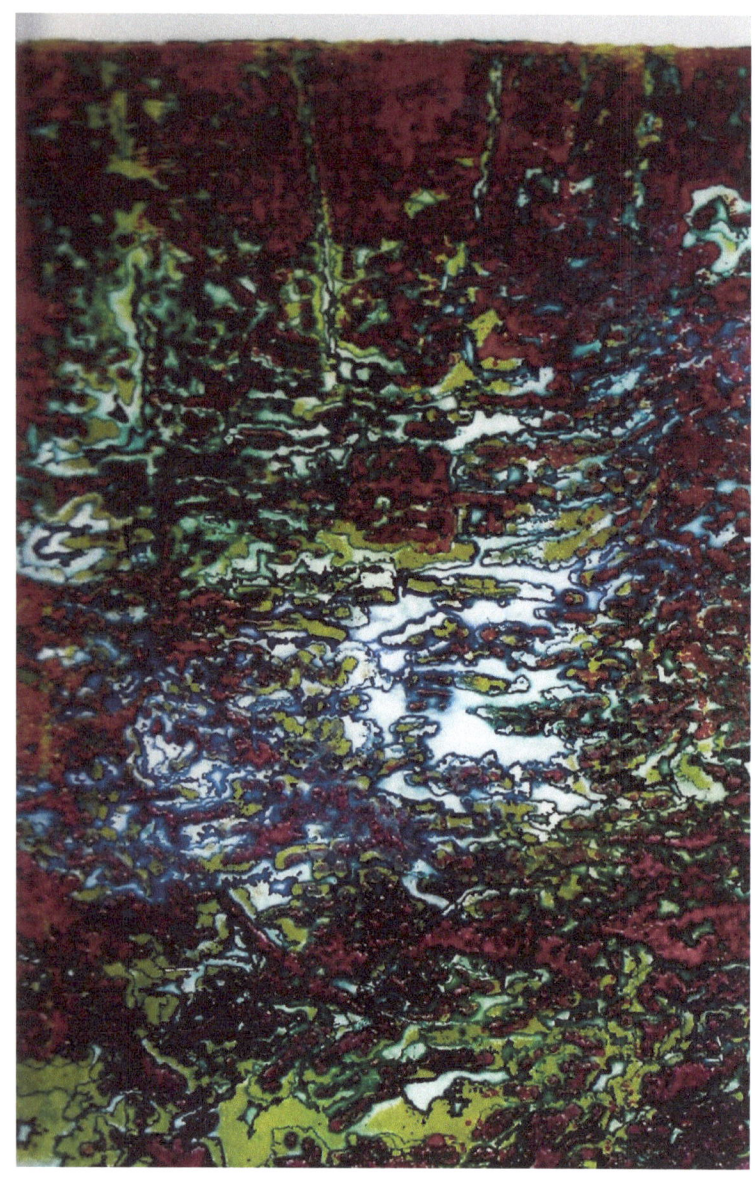

Fig 38 'Illusion.' No 30.   Viscosity print.

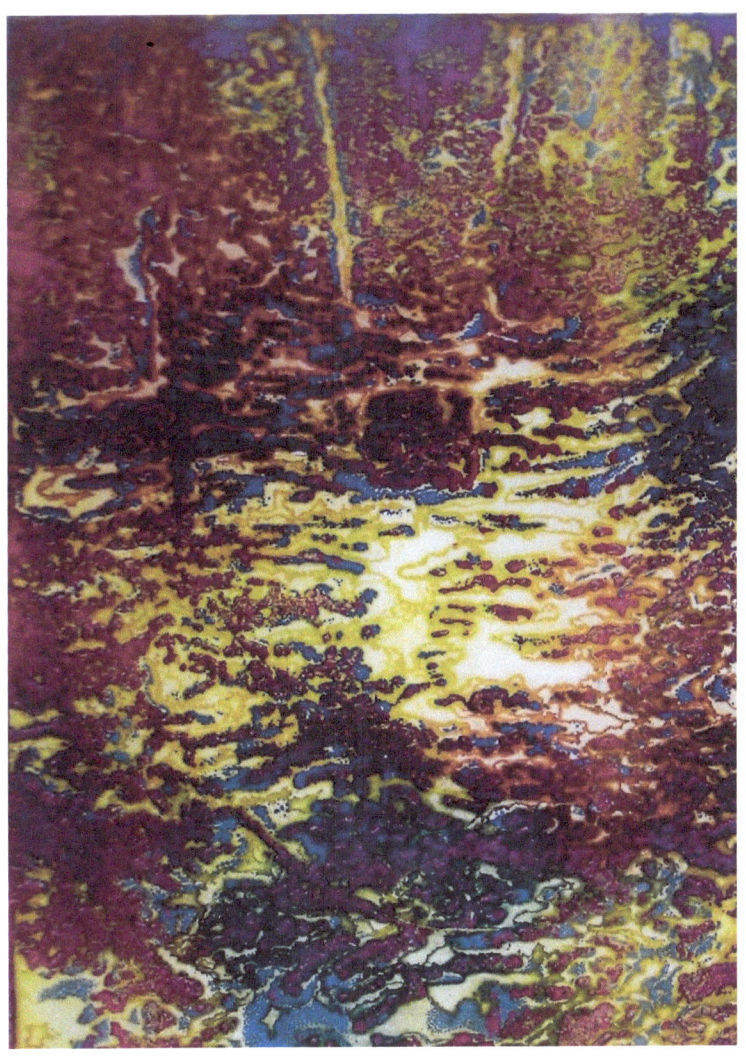

Fig 39 'Illusion.' No31 Viscosity print.

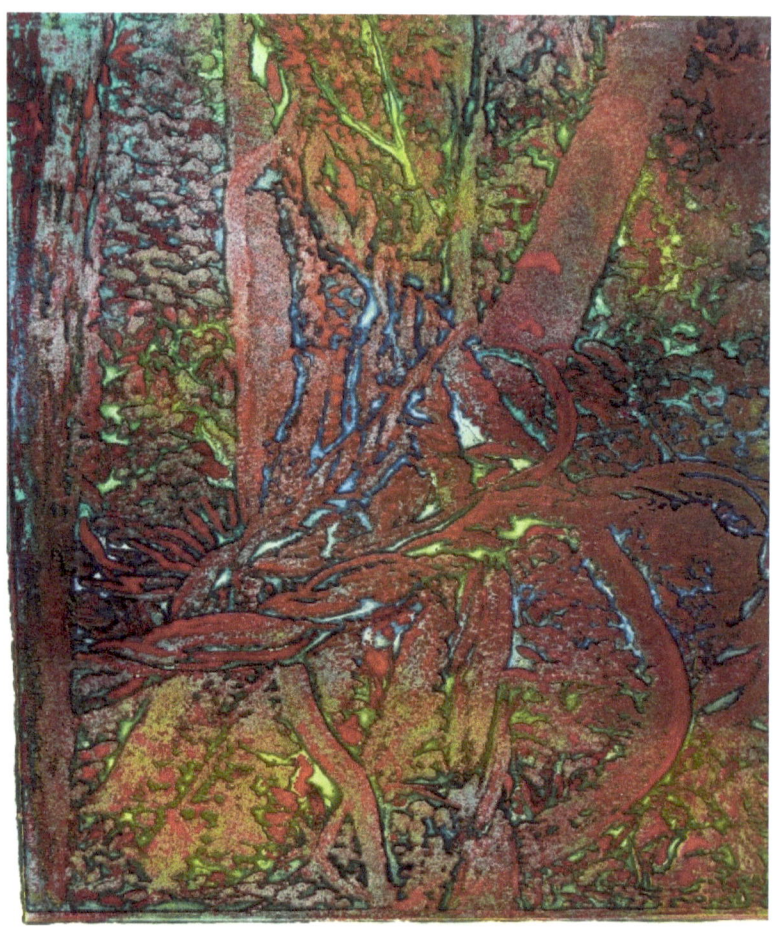

Fig 40 'Merely a Transition.' Viscosity print.

I was thrilled when another member of the public announced the work was communicating love and that we were both open and that there were others out there like us. Another was 'moved' by the work, then someone commented it was a Renaissance, creativity in the widest sense. Even the external assessor revisited in an unofficial capacity, in order to enjoy the ambiance of the show, 'More an experience rather than an exhibition.'

It was very encouraging to hear such positive comments from the public because this endorsed my aspiration of constructing a healing, meditative environment, suitable for hospitals, spars, hospices and natural museums, or even most public spaces in airports, corporate hotels, large offices etc.

I was fortunate to secure commissions at a nearby hospital and other commissions too, both being cancelled due to their finances, then the offer of a solo exhibition in the National Gallery, Beijing, China. Unfortunately, I was unable to secure funding for the trip. However, my ideas are many and I have not lost the desire to communicate creatively the knowledge I have acquired on my journey. I still intend to further my artwork, once my book is complete.

Another time in my life, I produced a piece of artwork for a client, who then proceeded to change the work a few times. It was completely ruined after those adjustments and the client withdrew from the commission because he too no longer liked it. This was a great lesson to me, to stay true to yourself and the interpretation of your intuition, refusing to be swayed by some other person or external interference.

I am aware of a shift in my art work, from becoming spiritually aware within the forest environment, to now incorporating my artwork to create healing environments, while now even being drawn towards sound, to increase the sensual experience. It is interesting to contemplate, as I move towards healing myself, I am also trying to heal others and the planet too.

It has now been scientifically proven the healing properties of being in nature, with tree hugging increasing the hormone oxytocin, which induces a feeling of calm and emotional bonding. Also, released is serotonin and dopamine, which makes us feel much happier. Meanwhile, the earthy smell of the forest floor, releases phytoncides, which lower the heart rate, reduces blood pressure and boosts the immune system.

As I progress on my journey, I have become more interested in sound being a vehicle for healing. Within the forest, there is the sound of the variety of birdsong, all competing for a solo performance, the running, gurgling of water, trickling over stones in the stream, the rustling of leaves in the trees, to the rhythm of the gusts of wind, the humming of the bees, as they gather nectar from the flowers. I find the birdsong of early Springtime a most spiritual experience. There are so many sounds in nature, if we only take time out to listen. This sound is very powerful and makes my heart sing. Everything in nature sings and vibrates in harmony, natures music. I believe there is a connection to spirit and soul, with each natural sound in nature, triggering vibrations in the atmosphere, while in turn, having a profound effect on man. Music is a force, giving off certain vibrations, depending on the type of sound.

I do so hope I have the opportunity to continue my artwork this time around, but if it is not the case, I am fairly sure I will be able to continue my work 'over the other side', since I am aware I learned many of my present skills during a past life.

On a practical level, I have noticed certain projects take much longer than originally anticipated. Within my artwork, I have a germ of an idea and it may take years to come to fruition. This is partly because I need to grow and mature, to take on board more of life's experiences along the way, before continuing on my quest.

Presently, I have been contemplating about a piece of work for almost twenty years, but during this time, I have been working towards my goal when producing a wide variety of experimental pieces, while maintaining my vision.

Our minds collate information from both inside and outside. For example, from a new thought, we are inspired to have a creative response, or we respond intuitively to our emotions when feeling happy or in love. I know when I have been having a new idea formulating around my head, it maybe a year or so before I become so enthused and excited about the prospect of the concept, so I am compelled to create the artwork. This mind work is looking for inspiration both externally and internally.

Sometimes, although I have tried to stay focused on my future plans as an artist, somehow, something has happened to 'block' the outcome. For example, I have had an invitation for a solo exhibition at an international gallery and yet I was unable to gain sponsorship or funding. Another time I gained a commission to produce a film in the main atrium of a hospital and yet the architect made an error and so the art budget was used to rectify his problem. Hence, my commission was cancelled. Those are just a few of the disappointments I have endured along the way, but I realise now that I was gently being 'held back' as I was being guided along my path in this life. I was not a failure. If it is meant to be that I have the opportunity to complete those projects, then things will fall into place at the right time for me. While we are here, we are not able to see the overall grand scheme of things. Once again, I need to acknowledge the gift of patience, to relax and let things run its course, rather than trying to force the issue. I find this task is so difficult for me as my enthusiasm and drive take over, which inevitably leads to frustration when events do not turn out as I had planned. I must keep my ego in check and stop trying to force an issue and trust the universe because all is well. I am safe and all things are following the grand plan, when everything will become clear to us in time. This applies to all of us and what we learn in this lifetime, we take this knowledge with us. I believe there are many dimensions where we as humans exist, where time is not as we know it. Here on earth is just a succession of lessons to learn, before we move forward on our way.

www.ingramcontent.com/pod-product-compliance
Lightning Source LLC
Chambersburg PA
CBHW040237220526
45473CB00001B/272